Elliott Carter

La Musique

Solo Soprano

Archive Edition

HENDON MUSIC

DISTRIBUTED BY

7777 W. BLUEMOUND RD. P.O. BOX 13819 MILWAUKEE, WI 53213

www.boosey.com
www.halleonard.com

First performed by Lucy Shelton on October 19, 2007
at the conference "The Flowering of Baudelaire"
(in commemoration of the 150th anniversary of publication of *Les Fleurs du Mal*)
Grant Recital Hall, Brown University, Providence, RI

COMPOSER'S NOTE

La Musique, for solo voice, is a short commemoration of the 150th anniversary of the
publication of Baudelaire's *Les Fleurs du Mal* in 1857, and is taken from that book of poems.

The piece is a small addition to the recital Lucy Shelton was to give of settings of Baudelaire
for that occasion and is dedicated to her.

– Elliott Carter
8/1/07

Duration: ca. 2 minutes

for Lucy Shelton

LA MUSIQUE
for Soprano

BAUDELAIRE

ELLIOTT CARTER
(2007)

New York, 24 June 2007